CRAFT TOPICS

DINOSAURS

FACTS • THINGS TO MAKE • ACTIVITIES

DAVID LAMBERT
and
RACHEL WRIGHT
Illustrations by Dale E. Evans

W
FRANKLIN WATTS
LONDON • SYDNEY

This edition 2006

First Published in Great Britain by
Franklin Watts
338 Euston Road
London NW1 3BH

Franklin Watts Australia
Hachette Children's Books
Level 17/207 Kent St
Sydney NSW 2000

Copyright © 1991 Franklin Watts

ISBN: 0 7496 6712 5
Dewey classification: 567.9

Editor: Hazel Poole
Designer: Sally Boothroyd
Photographer: Chris Fairclough

A CIP record for this book is available from the British Library.

Printed in Dubai, UAE

CONTENTS

WHAT WERE DINOSAURS?

Dinosaurs, or "terrible lizards", were prehistoric reptiles. Some grew bigger than an elephant, others no larger than a cat.

Dinosaurs were not like any reptiles now living. They did have tough, scaly skin and a long tail like a lizard. But they did not move like lizards. They stood, walked and ran like a horse or ostrich.

There were dinosaur plant-eaters and meat-eaters. Meat-eaters mainly had sharp teeth and claws. Plant-eaters either had blunt teeth or a toothless beak and ridged cheek teeth used for grinding leaves. Keen eyes and ears, and a good sense of smell warned dinosaurs of danger.

TWO GROUPS

Dinosaurs formed two great groups:
Saurischians ("lizard-hipped") had hip bones pointing in different directions, like a lizard's. All the flesh-eating dinosaurs and the largest of the plant-eating dinosaurs belonged to this group.

Ornithischians ("bird-hipped") had hip bones lying together and pointing in the same direction, like those of a bird. There were plated, armoured, horned, bird-footed and bone-headed ornithischians. All of them ate plants.

Hip Bones

Saurischian

Ornithischian

HOW DINOSAURS BEGAN

Active little reptiles, no bigger than rabbits, were alive about 230 million years ago. These lagosuchids ("rabbit crocodiles") were built rather like rabbits. But they were hunters. They walked on all fours, but might have run on their long hind limbs to catch small creatures in their jaws.

It is likely that the first dinosaurs came from lagosuchids. These first dinosaurs were sharp-toothed hunters. Some grew longer than a man although they weighed no more than a big dog.

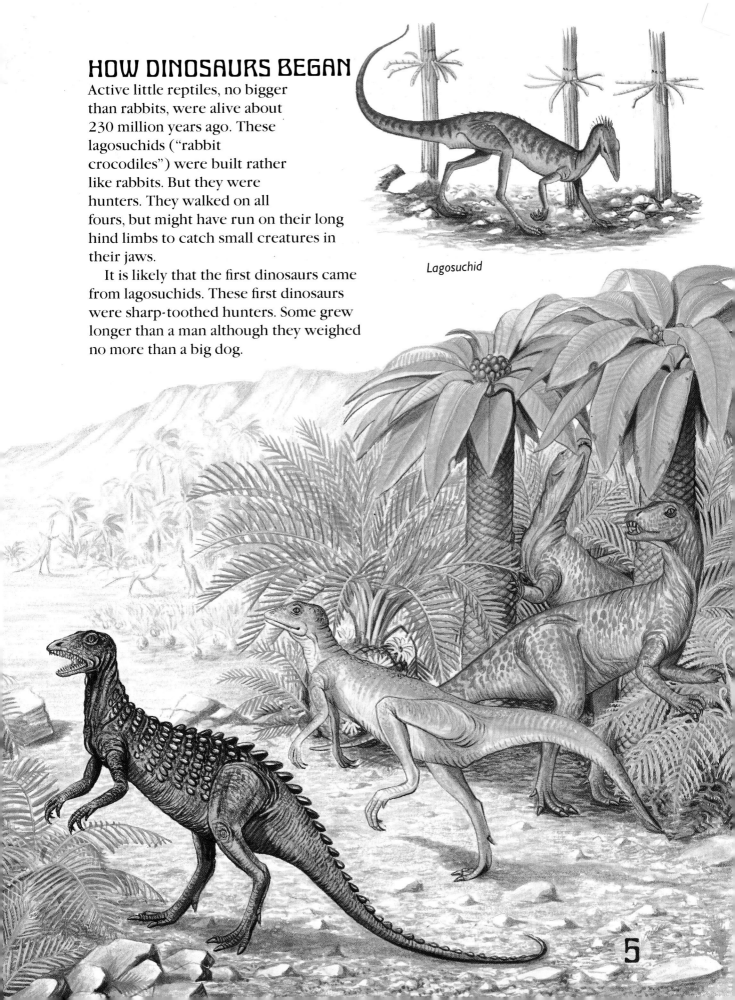

Lagosuchid

DINOSAUR TIMES

Dinosaurs appeared about 230 million years ago and quickly spread around the world. For 160 million years, they ruled the land. Then, mysteriously, they all died out.

TRIASSIC TIMES

This was the first part of the Age of Dinosaurs. At this time, all the land formed one large, warm and dry supercontinent. Early dinosaurs simply walked across the world! These reptiles grew no heavier than a large dog, yet from these there developed predators as heavy as cows, and plant-eaters the size of a bus. The plant-eating dinosaurs were the biggest Triassic land animals.

JURASSIC TIMES

The Jurassic Period was the middle of the Age of Dinosaurs. Fern meadows, palm-like cycadeoids, and tall conifers flourished along river banks. The southern land masses had just begun drifting apart, but not far enough to stop brand new kinds of dinosaur from spreading. Four-legged plant-eaters grew protective bony plates or spikes, or evolved into the immense sauropods. Their enemies included allosaurs: large predators with huge, sharp-fanged jaws. There were smaller dinosaurs too: plant-eaters and one sort of hunter that was not much bigger than a chicken.

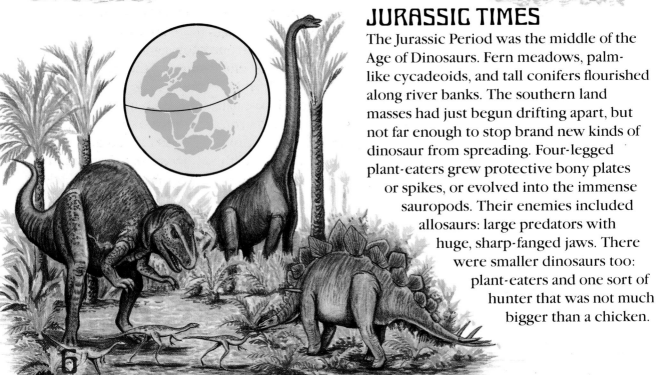

CRETACEOUS TIMES

The long Cretaceous Period ended the Age of Dinosaurs. Flowering plants appeared and ocean gaps widened. The climate was changing. There were more and stranger dinosaurs than ever before. North America had toothless ostrich dinosaurs, great duckbilled dinosaurs, rhinoceros-like, horned dinosaurs, and large armoured dinosaurs encased in bony plates. Tyrannosaurs, flesh-eating dinosaurs which weighed as much as an elephant, killed and ate these others when they could.

WHY THEY DISAPPEARED

About 65 million years ago, dinosaurs died out, along with most other large reptiles. Though there are many theories, no one knows why. Perhaps a thick dust cloud shut out the Sun's warmth and they froze to death. That could have happened if a huge rock or meteorite crashed into the Earth or a great many volcanoes blasted dust into the sky. Without dinosaurs to keep their numbers down, birds and mammals quickly multiplied.

CREATE YOUR OWN PREHISTORIC LANDSCAPE

You will need: 250g plain white flour • 125g salt • 2 tablespoons of cooking oil • water • mixing bowl • water-based paints • fuse wire • wire cutters • pliers • PVA glue • paper or coloured card • scissors • foil • baking sheet.

Ask an adult to help you.

1. Mix the flour and salt in a bowl. Pour in the oil and enough water to make a non-sticky dough. Cover your hands with flour and knead the dough well.

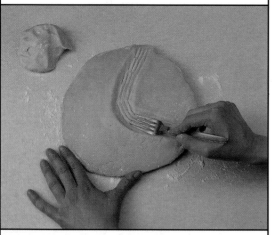

▲ **2.** Mould the dough into a landscape. Make extra details, such as cycadeoid trunks, too. Try using different objects, such as forks and spoons, to give your models texture.

3. Line a baking sheet with foil, and bake your landscape in the bottom of the oven on gas mark 4 (350°F/180°C) for about 25 minutes.

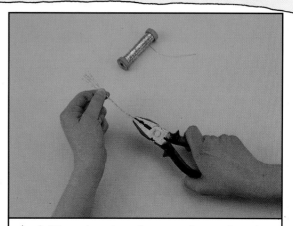

▲ **4.** To make giant ferns and cycadeoid leaves, twist lengths of fuse wire together. It helps if you grip the wires with a pair of pliers at one end, and twist holding the other end.

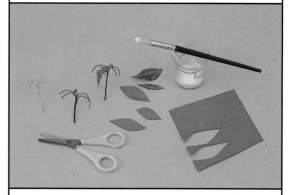

▲ **5.** Separate the wires at the top, and bend them slightly. Now paint your wire frame.
  Cut fern-like leaves from card or painted paper, and glue each leaf on its wire stem.

6. Decide which types of conifer you want to make, then follow either steps 7-9 or step 10.

7. Twist lengths of wire together, as in step 4.

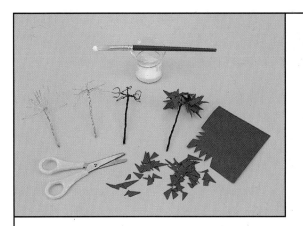

8. Separate the wires at the top of the tree. Now twist some of these wire strands together, to create branches.

Bend the tip of each branch inwards, and paint the tree frame.

9. Cut pointed leaves from card or painted paper. Cover the branch tips with glue, and sprinkle the leaves over them.

10. To make conifers such as yew trees, cut strands of wire of equal length, and start twisting them together.

Once the trunk is long enough, separate about four strands of wire, as shown.

Continue twisting upwards, separating wire strands as you go.

When your tree is the right height, paint it. If you are not happy with its shape, trim and bend the branches.

Cover the branches with glue and sprinkle them with needle-shaped leaves cut from paper.

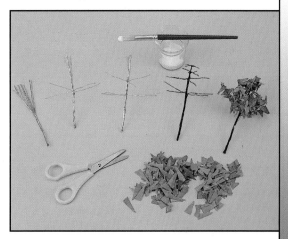

11. When your dough landscape has cooled, paint it. Push your wire trees into the dough, and your cycadeoid leaves into their trunks.

Flesh-Eaters

All meat-eating dinosaurs belonged to a group called *Theropoda* ("beast foot"). They were built like birds, but most had scaly skin, sharp teeth and claws, and a bony tail.

DEINONYCHUS

"Terrible claw" was, perhaps, the most terrifying meat-eating dinosaur of all. It had a long, sharp, curved claw on each second toe which was held up out of the way when it walked. To grapple with an enemy, it stood on one leg, balanced by its long stiff tail. Then it kicked hard. The claw swung forward, ripping open the victim's belly. *Deinonychus* was only 3 metres long, but a pack of them could kill much bigger dinosaurs.

STRUTHIOMIMUS

In a dim light, *Struthiomimus* ("ostrich mimic") would have looked like an ostrich as it lowered its long neck to peck at plants or insects with a toothless beak. Ornithomimids ("bird mimics") like this may have had bare skin, a bony tail, long arms, and three-fingered hands with claws. *Struthiomimus's* big, keen eyes kept a sharp watch for danger. It could kick enemies hard or outrun them.

COMPSOGNATHUS

"Pretty jaw" grew scarcely bigger than a chicken. This was a fierce little hunter, which snapped up any lizards it could catch. One fossil *Compsognathus* was found with a swallowed lizard still inside!

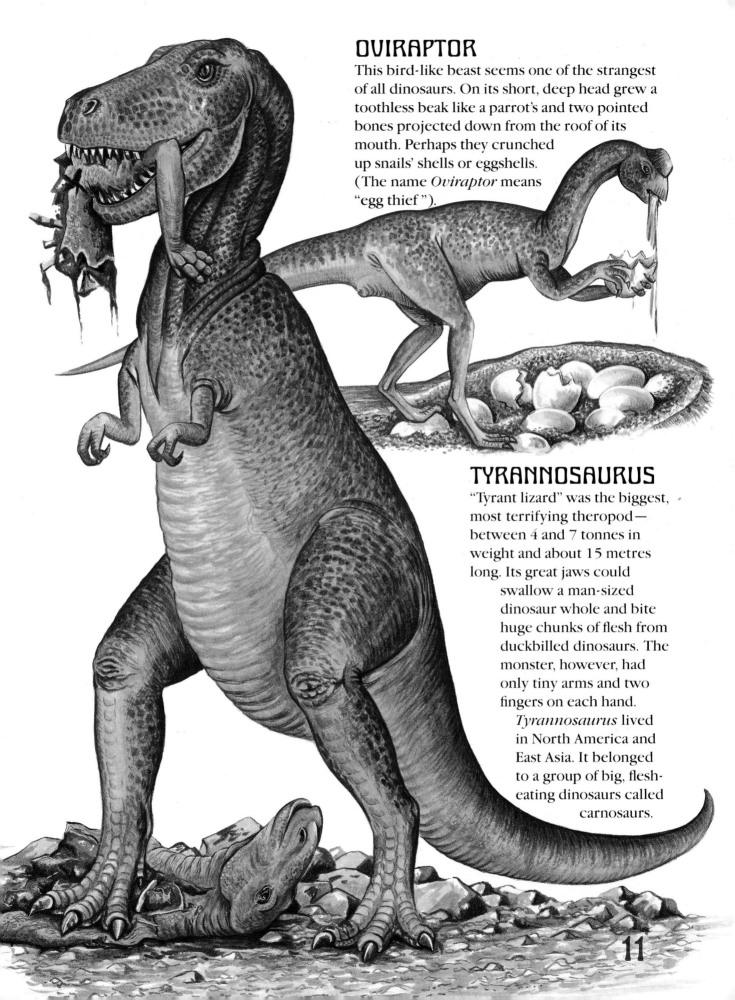

OVIRAPTOR

This bird-like beast seems one of the strangest of all dinosaurs. On its short, deep head grew a toothless beak like a parrot's and two pointed bones projected down from the roof of its mouth. Perhaps they crunched up snails' shells or eggshells. (The name *Oviraptor* means "egg thief").

TYRANNOSAURUS

"Tyrant lizard" was the biggest, most terrifying theropod— between 4 and 7 tonnes in weight and about 15 metres long. Its great jaws could swallow a man-sized dinosaur whole and bite huge chunks of flesh from duckbilled dinosaurs. The monster, however, had only tiny arms and two fingers on each hand.

Tyrannosaurus lived in North America and East Asia. It belonged to a group of big, flesh-eating dinosaurs called carnosaurs.

11

BIG AND SPEEDY PLANT-EATERS

These two pages show two lizard-hipped and two bird-hipped kinds of plant-eaters. These peaceful creatures relied mainly on size or speed to save them from the meat-eating theropods.

PLATEOSAURUS

"Flat lizard" grew up to 8 metres long and belonged to the lizard-hipped prosauropods ("before the sauropods"). Its body was heavy and the neck and tail were long. Leaf-shaped teeth shredded leaves for digesting in the creature's bulky stomach. *Plateosaurus* could rear up to jab its big, curved thumb claws at an enemy.

BRACHIOSAURUS

"Arm lizard" was the largest well-known sauropod. Almost three bus-lengths long, it weighed as much as eight elephants. At its full height this monster stood about 12 metres tall. It lived in North America and Africa 150 million years ago.

APATOSAURUS

"Deceptive lizard" is often known as *Brontosaurus* ("thunder lizard") because scientists thought its pillar-like legs must have shaken the ground as it walked. *Apatosaurus* weighed as much as 30 tonnes and grew to 21 metres long, but much of this length was neck and tail. Some other sauropods ("lizard feet") grew longer and heavier.

IGUANODON

"Iguana tooth" cropped leaves with its toothless beak, and chewed them up with cheek teeth which were similar to an iguana lizard's, but far larger. It measured 9 metres long and weighed about 5 tonnes. Big bird-hipped ornithopods ("bird foot" dinosaurs) like *Iguanodon* and the duckbilled dinosaurs plodded on all fours, but ran on their long, strong hind limbs. Spiky thumbs were *Iguanodon's* only weapons.

PACHYCEPHALOSAURUS

"Thick-headed lizard" was a bird-hipped dinosaur with a thick bony skull like a crash helmet. Their dome-shaped skulls protected their brains when two male bone-headed dinosaurs head-butted each other.

MODEL A STEGOSAURUS

Newspaper pulp modelling can be messy. You may need to tape a plastic sheet or bag over your surface before you start.

You will need: a large plastic bag • a bowl of warm water • wallpaper paste • glue brush • newspaper • water-based paints • cocktail sticks • scissors • cardboard • strong glue.

1. Soak a sheet of newspaper in warm water. Squeeze out the excess water, trying not to tear the paper.

4. If parts of your model start to droop, try pushing cocktail sticks into the pulp to hold it firm.

5. Leave the body and legs in a warm place to dry. If your model is quite large, this may take a day or two.

▲ **2.** Lay the paper flat and coat one side of it with wallpaper paste. Scrunch the pasted paper into a ball and knead it into a pulp. Repeat this until you have enough newspaper pulp to work with.

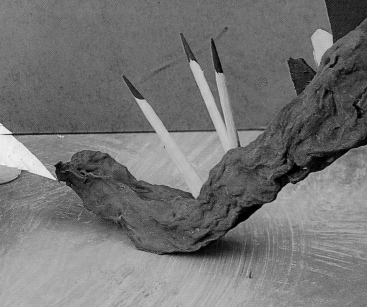

▲ **3.** Model the body of your *Stegosaurus* first, and make the legs separately. Make sure that the legs are the right height and width to support the body.

◀ **6.** Cut spine plates out of cardboard and paint them. Paint some cocktail sticks for tail spikes, too.

7. When all the various parts of your model are dry, paint the body and legs, and glue everything into place.

People once thought *Stegosaurus* had a second brain, in its back. This was really a bulge in the spinal cord that sent signals to and from its brain.

ARMOURED PLANT-EATERS

These two pages show one each of four kinds of four-legged ornithischians. Spikes or armour protected these plant-eaters against the theropods.

SCELIDOSAURUS

"Limb lizard" grew as long as a car, with four sturdy legs, a low head, and a heavy body and long tail. Its lightweight armour was made of rounded scales and rows of bony studs or cones. Early scelidosaurs like this one might have given rise to the plated and armoured dinosaurs.

ANKYLOSAURUS

"Fused lizard" looked like an armoured car on legs, about 10 metres long! It was as well protected as any armadillo or tortoise. A carnosaur that bit an *Ankylosaurus* risked breaking its teeth on the bony plates and spikes set in the armoured dinosaur's tough skin. This beast could also hit its enemies with its heavy tail, which ended in a bony club as big as a man's head.

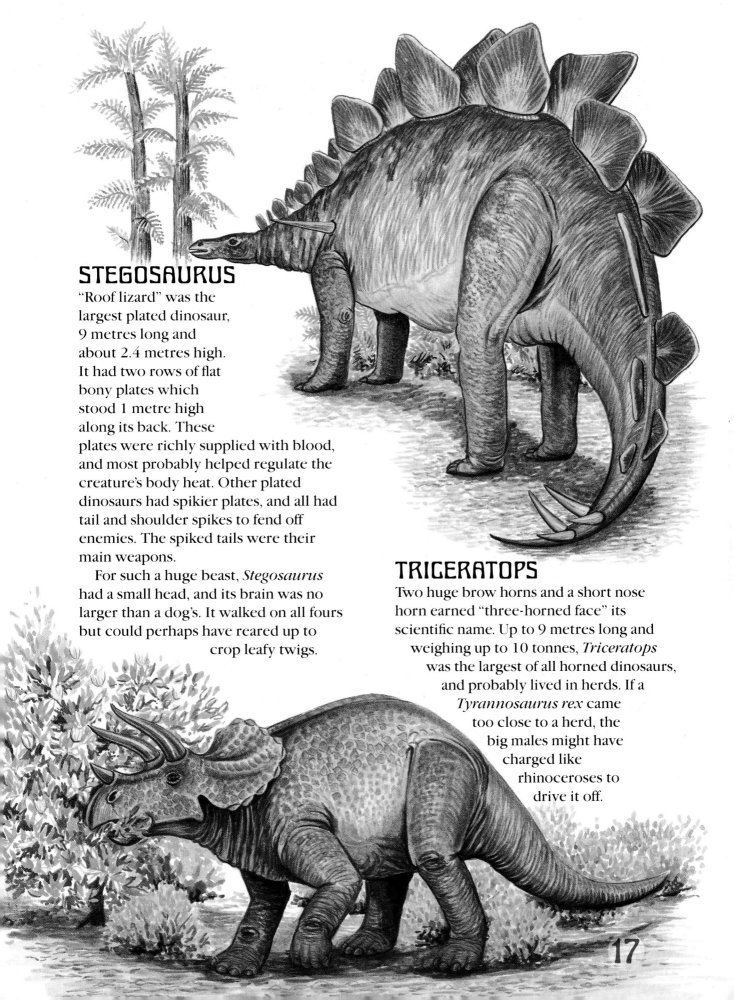

STEGOSAURUS

"Roof lizard" was the largest plated dinosaur, 9 metres long and about 2.4 metres high. It had two rows of flat bony plates which stood 1 metre high along its back. These plates were richly supplied with blood, and most probably helped regulate the creature's body heat. Other plated dinosaurs had spikier plates, and all had tail and shoulder spikes to fend off enemies. The spiked tails were their main weapons.

For such a huge beast, *Stegosaurus* had a small head, and its brain was no larger than a dog's. It walked on all fours but could perhaps have reared up to crop leafy twigs.

TRICERATOPS

Two huge brow horns and a short nose horn earned "three-horned face" its scientific name. Up to 9 metres long and weighing up to 10 tonnes, *Triceratops* was the largest of all horned dinosaurs, and probably lived in herds. If a *Tyrannosaurus rex* came too close to a herd, the big males might have charged like rhinoceroses to drive it off.

17

BECOME A TRICERATOPS

Ask an adult to help you.

You will need: 1 metre of narrow gauge chicken wire • wire cutters • newspaper • wallpaper paste • glue brush • scissors • elastic • water-based paints • ruler.

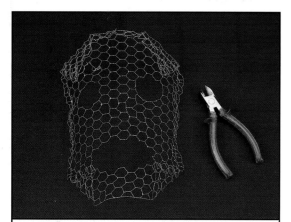

▲ **1.** Cut a square of chicken wire 30 × 30cm. Fold back the edges, and shape the wire to fit your face. Cut holes for your mouth and eyes.

▲ **2.** To make the nose, cut a piece of wire 30 × 10cm. Snip away at one of the longer edges so that it comes to a point in the middle.

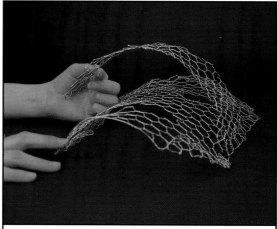

▲ **3.** Curve the nose piece slightly, and attach it by twisting its jagged wire ends into the sides of your mask.

▲ **4.** Cut out three small triangles of wire. Twist each one into a horn, and fix them to the mask, in the same way you fastened the nose.

▲ **5.** To make the forehead, cut a rectangle of wire about 20 × 10cm. Attach it lengthwise to the nose and the top of the mask.

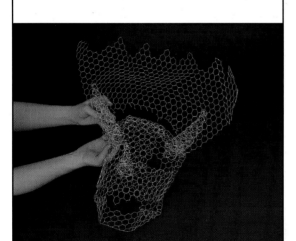

▲ **6.** To make the neck frill, cut a piece of wire about 55 × 30cm. Snip away the corners, and cut a zigzag along one of the longer edges.

　　Bend the opposite edge into a curve, and fasten it to the top of your mask.

7. Cover the whole mask, outside and inside, with layers of newspaper, coated in wallpaper paste. You will need about six layers in all. Let each layer dry thoroughly before you apply the next.

▲ **8.** Using a pair of scissors, pierce a hole at the top and on each side of the mask. Thread a length of strong elastic through each hole, and tie all three lengths together at the back. Now paint your mask, and frighten your friends!

Triceratops males had big, long-horned skulls. Smaller skulls with shorter horns came from *Triceratops* females and young.

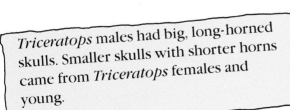

DINOSAUR LIFE

MOVING ABOUT

Fossil footprints show us how dinosaurs walked, ran, and swam. Narrow tracks tell us they walked with their legs erect, not sprawling. Long gaps between footprints show that a two-legged dinosaur ran as fast as a galloping horse. Two front foot fossil footprints are the marks left where a sauropod kicked off as it swam across a lake. Side-by-side tracks show where a herd of sauropods passed by.

Length of stride

FEEDING

Flesh-eaters had curved, pointed teeth like knife blades. These bit off chunks of meat as if they were soft butter. A sauropod's chisel-shaped or spoon-shaped teeth cropped fern fronds and tree leaves. Deliberately swallowed "gizzard stones" — called gastroliths — in its stomach crushed the leaves, and bacteria helped digest them. Ornithischians snipped off leaves with a horny beak and chewed them with leaf-shaped cheek teeth — as many as 700 in a duckbilled dinosaur.

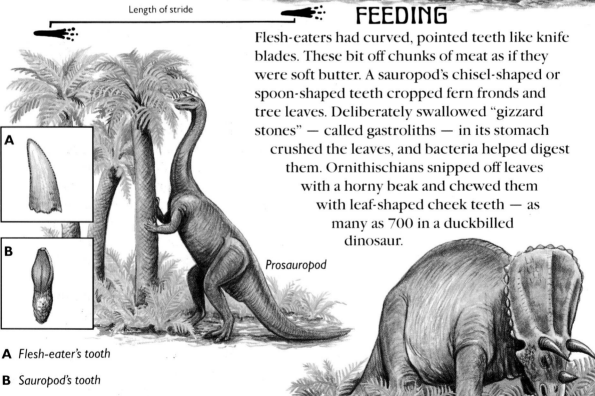

A

B

Prosauropod

A *Flesh-eater's tooth*

B *Sauropod's tooth*

Horned dinosaur

FIGHTING

Big theropods attacked with gaping jaws. Small theropods seized prey in their hands or kicked out with clawed toes. Under attack, a sauropod might jab with its sharp thumb claws, or rear up and crash down on an enemy. Plated and armoured dinosaurs and some sauropods could lash out with their tails. Perhaps horned dinosaurs drove their horns deep into an enemy.

A theropod attacks

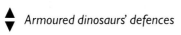

▲ ▼ Armoured dinosaurs' defences

RAISING A FAMILY

Dinosaur babies hatched from eggs that were laid in holes dug in sand or in mud nests built on the ground. The biggest eggs were not much larger than ostrich eggs. Mothers very likely covered up their eggs until the Sun's warmth hatched them. Some mothers guarded their eggs and babies against egg-eating dinosaurs. *Maiasaura* ("good mother lizard") even brought food to her young before they left their nest.

Maiasaura's nest

Fly A Reptile

Dinosaurs couldn't fly, but their reptile relatives, the pterosaurs could!

▲ **1.** Cut a piece of card 40 × 10cm. Fold it in half. Draw a head shape on one side, and cut it out. Take care not to cut into the fold.

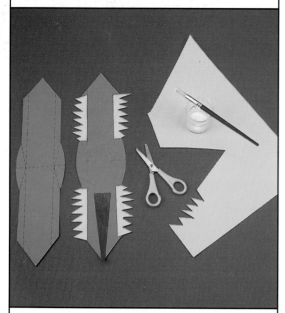

▲ **2.** Open the card and mark it as shown.

3. Make some card teeth and a tongue and glue them into place.

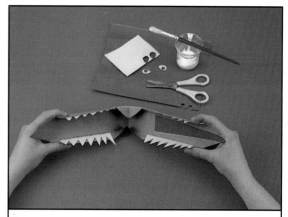

▲ **4.** To complete the head, fold all the broken lines you've drawn inwards. Add two eyes, cut from the card.

▲ **5.** To make the body, roll a piece of card 30 × 20 cm into a tube. Stick it together with glue.

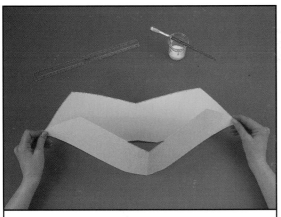

▲ **6.** Cut two sets of wings, each measuring about 60cm across. Glue both sets of wings together at their tips.

▲ **7.** To make each limb, intertwine three pipe cleaners, leaving a claw at one end.
 When you've made four limbs, glue them to the underside of the wings.

▲ **8.** To make the tail, cut three identical card shapes. Glue them together at their tips, and add a kite-shaped rudder.

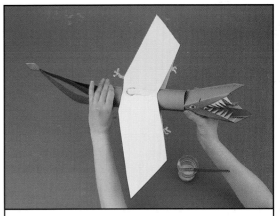

▲ **9.** Tape a curtain ring to the top of the wings. Slip the wings over the body tube, and glue to secure. Glue the three tail pieces into one end of the tube, and the head into the other.

10. Hang some string from a wall hook, and thread both ends through the curtain ring. Pull the two loose ends apart, and watch as your reptile whizzes through the air.

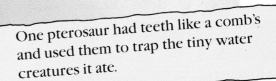

One pterosaur had teeth like a comb's and used them to trap the tiny water creatures it ate.

Fossil Dinosaurs

We know about dinosaurs thanks to the remains of their bodies that have been discovered preserved in rocks as fossils. Dinosaur fossils can be bones, teeth, skin, eggs, footprints — even droppings.

HOW FOSSILS FORM

Dead dinosaurs usually rotted away in the open air, but sometimes a corpse sank in a lake or river. Mud covering its bones protected them against decay. Dissolved minerals filled tiny holes in the bones, gradually turning them to fossils. Once fossilized, they were strong enough to resist the weight of mud piling up above and hardening into layered rocks. Hardened mud held fossil footprints too. Some fossils are hollows left where dinosaur bones dissolved away. These fossil hollows are called moulds. Moulds that became filled in with minerals are called casts.

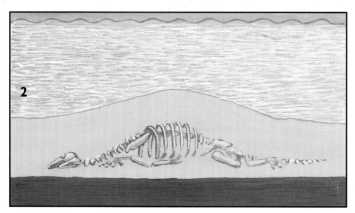

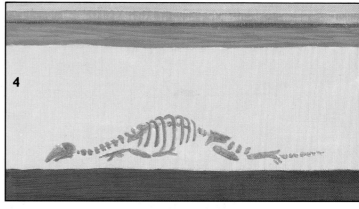

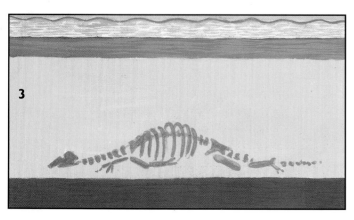

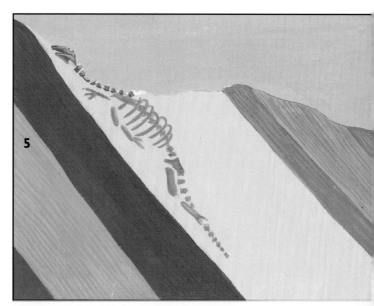

FINDING FOSSILS

Dinosaur hunters search layered rocks formed in the Age of Dinosaurs. They look where rocks have been forced up as hills. Rain wears away hill slopes, laying bare the fossil bones within. The best hunting grounds are often cliffs and deserts.

The fossil hunters search for clues low down on slopes. A thumb-sized shiny lump of "stone" might be a fossil washed down from the hill above. Higher up, a whole skeleton might still lie stuck in rock.

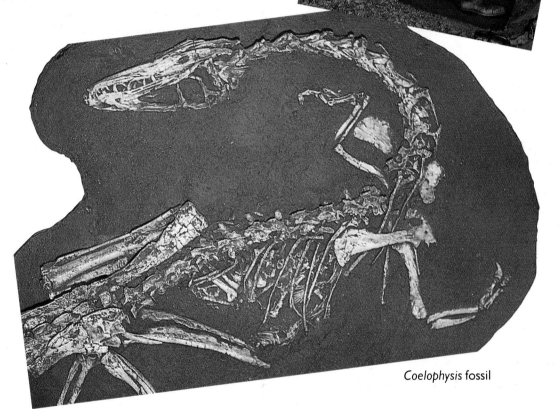

Coelophysis fossil

DIGGING UP DINOSAURS

A team of people can take weeks to dig up a big fossil dinosaur. Bulldozers and power-hammers might strip off the outer rocks, but removing stone from around brittle bones needs careful work with finer tools like chisels. The team photographs and numbers the bones, packs them carefully, then takes them to a museum.

IN THE MUSEUM

Inside the museum, experts clean the dinosaur bones. Next they work out how the bones once fitted together. Then they can rebuild the skeleton. Clamps and metal rods hold the bones in place.

Looking at a dinosaur's skeleton helps an artist to picture the animal with its covering of flesh and skin.

MAKE YOUR OWN FOSSILS

You will need: an object to fossilize, such as a leaf or shell • plasticine • an old rolling pin • cooking oil • pastry brush • thin card • scissors • plaster of Paris • water • mixing bowl • knife • tape.

▲ **1.** Smooth a slab of plasticine with a rolling pin. Press the object you want to "fossilize" firmly into the plasticine.

2. Remove the object carefully, and brush the plasticine imprint it has made with a little cooking oil.

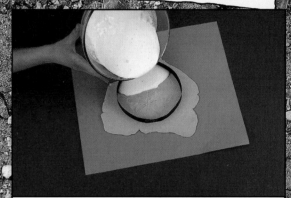

▲ **5.** Pour the plaster of Paris mixture into your card circle.

6. When the plaster of Paris is nearly dry, peel away the strip of card.

7. When the plaster of Paris is completely dry, remove the plasticine carefully, and paint your "fossil".

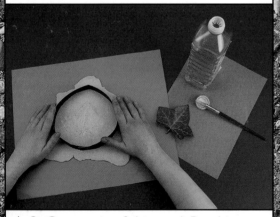

▲ **3.** Cut a strip of thin card. Bend it around your imprinted shape, and press it gently into the plasticine. Tape the ends of card together.

4. Mix one cup of plaster of Paris powder with half a cup of water, and stir well with a knife.

Dinosaur timechart

Years ago (millions)	SAURISCHIANS (lizard-hipped)			ORNITHISCHIANS (bird-hipped)
	THEROPODS (meat-eaters)	PROSAUROPODS (plant-eaters)	SAUROPODS (plant-eaters)	
65 CRETACEOUS	Tyrannosaurus Struthiomimus Oviraptor Deinonychus			Wannanosaurus Pachycephalosaurus Ankylosaurus Torosaurus Triceratops Maiasaura Iguanodon
144 JURASSIC	Compsognathus Megalosaurus		Brachiosaurus Apatosaurus (Brontosaurus) Mamenchisaurus	Stegosaurus Scelidosaurus
213 TRIASSIC **248**		Plateosaurus Mussaurus		

DID YOU KNOW?

Birds are the only living descendants of the dinosaurs. Birds developed from small flesh-eating dinosaurs with teeth and claws and long bony tails. The first known bird had all of these, but feathers, too. This crow-sized creature, known as *Archaeopteryx* ("ancient wing"), lived 150 million years ago. Modern birds lack teeth and bony tails but still have dinosaur-type legs, ankles and toes.

By 1990, scientists had named more than 500 kinds of dinosaur worldwide, but only about 280 were truly different kinds. One scientist believes there were about 1,000 different kinds altogether. Most have never been discovered. No more than 100 kinds would have been alive at the same time.

Archaeopteryx fossil

One of the largest known dinosaurs was an immense sauropod dug up in Argentina in 1989. Though only a few of its bones were found, these were enough to give an impression of the creature's size. Experts believe that the monster measured up to 35 metres long and weighed up to 80 tonnes. It belonged to the group of sauropods called titanosaurids ("giants").

◀ Another sauropod, *Mamenchisaurus*, from China, had the longest neck of any animal that ever lived.

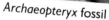

Several dinosaurs were tiny. One of the smallest of all was the Chinese bone-headed dinosaur *Wannanosaurus* ("Wannan lizard"). *Wannanosaurus* was no bigger than a chicken. Even smaller dinosaurs are known, but these were usually babies. You could have held a baby *Mussaurus* ("mouse lizard") in your hand. This Argentinian prosauropod hatched from an egg no larger than a sparrow's.

Fossil hunters have found more kinds of dinosaur in China and the United States than in any other countries. By 1990, scientists had named 110 kinds of dinosaur from the United States, and 95 from China. (Some of these dinosaurs lived in both places.) New finds from China seem likely to put that country in the lead.

The horned dinosaur *Torosaurus* ("bull lizard"), found in New Mexico, had a head as long as a car. It was the largest head of any animal that ever lived. Most of the head was a frill made of two long skull bones that stuck out backwards above the creature's neck.

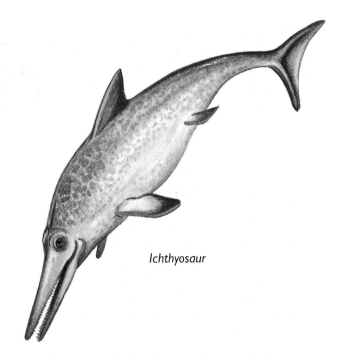

Ichthyosaur

Many people mistakenly think that the flying pterosaurs ("winged lizards"), swimming plesiosaurs ("near lizards") and ichthyosaurs ("fish lizards") were dinosaurs. These animals certainly lived at the same time as the dinosaurs, but there were no flying dinosaurs. Pterosaurs were only close relatives while plesiosaurs and ichthyosaurs belonged to a completely different group of reptiles.

Torosaurus

Glossary

Age of Dinosaurs — what scientists call the Mesozoic Era ("Age of Middle Life"). This lasted from 248 to 65 million years ago. The earliest dinosaurs we know of lived about 230 million years ago.

Allosaurs — big flesh-eating dinosaurs, part of the carnosaur group.

Armoured dinosaurs — four-legged ornithischians with bony armour.

Bone-headed dinosaurs — two-legged ornithischians with thick skulls.

Carnosaurs — big, flesh-eating theropods, such as *Allosaurus*, *Megalosaurus* and *Tyrannosaurus*.

Cast — fossil formed by a material filling in a hollow left by dinosaur remains that dissolved away.

Cretaceous — the last part of the Age of Dinosaurs, 144-65 million years ago.

Cycadeoids — stubby palm-like plants eaten by some kinds of dinosaurs.

Duckbilled dinosaurs — big ornithischian dinosaurs that walked on all fours, but hurried on their hind limbs. They had many cheek teeth, but toothless beaks.

Fossils — remains of ancient animals or plants preserved in rocks. They include bones, teeth, footprints, skin or droppings.

Gastroliths — stones or pebbles swallowed to help grind down food in the stomach.

Horned dinosaurs — four-legged ornithischians with horns. They were built rather like rhinoceroses.

Ichthyosaurs — not dinosaurs, but sea reptiles somewhat like dolphins.

Jurassic — the middle part of the Age of Dinosaurs, 213-144 million years ago.

Lagosuchids — small, lively Triassic reptiles. They were the ancestors of the dinosaurs and pterosaurs.

Ornithischians — dinosaurs with hip bones arranged like a bird's. All of them ate plants.

Ornithomimids — a family of toothless theropods rather resembling ostriches.

Ornithopods — a group of small and large two-legged ornithischians. Big ones like *Iguanodon* walked slowly on all fours.

Plated dinosaurs — four-legged ornithischians with bony plates or spikes sticking up along the back.

Plesiosaurs — not dinosaurs but big sea reptiles that swam with flippers.

Prosauropods — early saurischian plant-eaters with long necks and bulky bodies. They included the biggest early dinosaurs.

Pterosaurs — not dinosaurs but flying and gliding reptiles related to dinosaurs.

Reptiles — cold-blooded backboned animals including snakes and lizards.

Saurischians — dinosaurs with hip bones rather like a lizard's. They included the flesh-eating theropods and the plant-eating prosauropods and sauropods.

Sauropods — great four-legged plant-eating saurischians, with long necks and tails.

Scelidosaurids — a family of four-legged ornithischians that perhaps gave rise to the armoured and plated dinosaurs.

Theropods — flesh-eating saurischian dinosaurs. Some had huge jaws and fangs, others had no teeth at all.

Titanosaurids — a family of sauropods. The best-known kinds lived in South America.

Triassic — the first part of the Age of Dinosaurs, 248-213 million years ago.

Tyrannosaurids — a family of theropods. It included *Tyrannosaurus*, one of the biggest carnosaurs of all.

Warm-blooded — having a body temperature that stays constant even when the surroundings become cold or hot.

RESOURCES

PLACES TO VISIT
The Natural History Museum
Cromwell Road, London SW7 5BD
www.nhm.ac.uk
See dinosaur models, skeletons and eggs. The website is also informative and fun.

Dinosaur Farm Museum
Sandown, Isle of Wight
Tel: 01983 740401
www.dinosaur.farm.co.uk
This museum prides itself on having real dinosaur bones. You can find out about Isle of Wight dinosaurs and digs. There are also fossil hunts on the beaches.

Dinosaur Museum, Icen Way,
Dorchester, Dorset, Tel: 01305 269880
www.thedinosaurmuseum.com
Visit the museum and you will see dinosaur reconstructions – there are two tyrannosaurus rex, a stegosaurus, a corythosaurus, and a triceratops.

WEBSITES
www.dinosaursociety.com
This society has events through the year – keep up to date with the directory. The gallery of illustrations depicting dinosaurs is a great resource. You can also send in your own artwork of dinosaurs for the site.

www.paleojos.com
A great kids page with jokes and downloads to colour in. Go to the home page for information on fossils and more – you can even buy fossil teeth!

www.show.me.uk
Full of information, this site shows fun, cool, scary, wild, crazy stuff from the UK's museums and galleries. Search by topic, including dinosaurs, and you will find games, news, and places to go that are close to where you live.

Note to parents and teachers: Every effort has been made by the Publishers to ensure that the websites in this book are suitable for children, that they are of the highest educational value, and that they contain no inappropriate or offensive material. However, because of the nature of the Internet, it is impossible to guarantee that the contents of these sites will not be altered. We strongly advise that Internet access is supervised by a responsible adult.

INDEX